wal

fra

zier

by Larry Batson

illustrated by
Harold Henriksen

Amecus Street
Mankato, Minnesota 56001

Published by Amecus Street, 123 South Broad Street, P. O. Box 113, Mankato, Minnesota 56001
Copyright © 1974 by Amecus Street. International copyrights reserved in all countries.
No part of this book may be reproduced in any form without written permission from the publisher.
Printed in the United States.
Distributed by Childrens Press, 1224 West Van Buren Street, Chicago, Illinois 60607
Library of Congress Numbers: 74-2013   ISBN: 0-87191-348-8
Cover Photo by John E. Biever

Library of Congress Cataloging in Publication Data
Batson, Larry, 1930   Walt Frazier.

(Superstars)
SUMMARY: Follows the basketball career of "Clyde" Walt Frazier, star of the New York
"Knicks" whose skill in the sport has made him a millionaire.
1. Frazier, Walt, 1945-   —Juvenile literature. [1. Frazier, Walt, 1945-   2. Basketball—Biography]
I. Henriksen, Harold, illus. II. Title.
GV884.F7B37   796.32'3'0924 [B] [92]   74-2013   ISBN 0-87191-348-8

walt
frazier

His manner is cool and confident as he dribbles the basketball down the floor. He moves steadily and slowly. Then he blurs into action in a split-second when he sees an opening.

His face is always expressionless. His head tilts back a tiny bit. It's the pose of a gambler in a high-stakes game checking his opponents across the table. His eyes register every movement of the player guarding him and the actions of his teammates and the men guarding them.

Meanwhile, the 19,000 fans jammed into Madison Square Garden are roaring themselves hoarse. If the game is close or their beloved Knicks are losing, shouts of "Clyde, Clyde, Clyde" are deafening.

The man with the basketball is Walt Frazier,

superstar of the New York Knicks. He's the floor leader of the big city's team and, many observers feel, the finest all-round player in professional basketball today.

Certainly, New York fans would vote that way. They have seen the Knicks turn to Frazier for leadership or for the crucial play countless times. He is at his best when the pressure is greatest.

Most of those fans call Frazier "Clyde," a nickname bestowed because he likes the styles in clothes set by the movie, "Bonnie and Clyde." Before and after any Knicks game, you can wander through the crowd and hear a dozen stories of "Clyde's" greatest games. For instance, there was the night the Knicks were trying to win their 18th straight game, something no pro basketball team had ever done.

The Knicks were behind, 105 to 102, with just 16 seconds left to play. Their opponents, the Cincinnati Royals, had the ball out of bounds at midcourt. All the Royals had to do was pass the ball in and hold it until time ran out.

But the clock would not start running until somebody on the court touched the ball. Frazier knew that if he could prevent a safe, clean pass inbounds, there would be a chance for an interception.

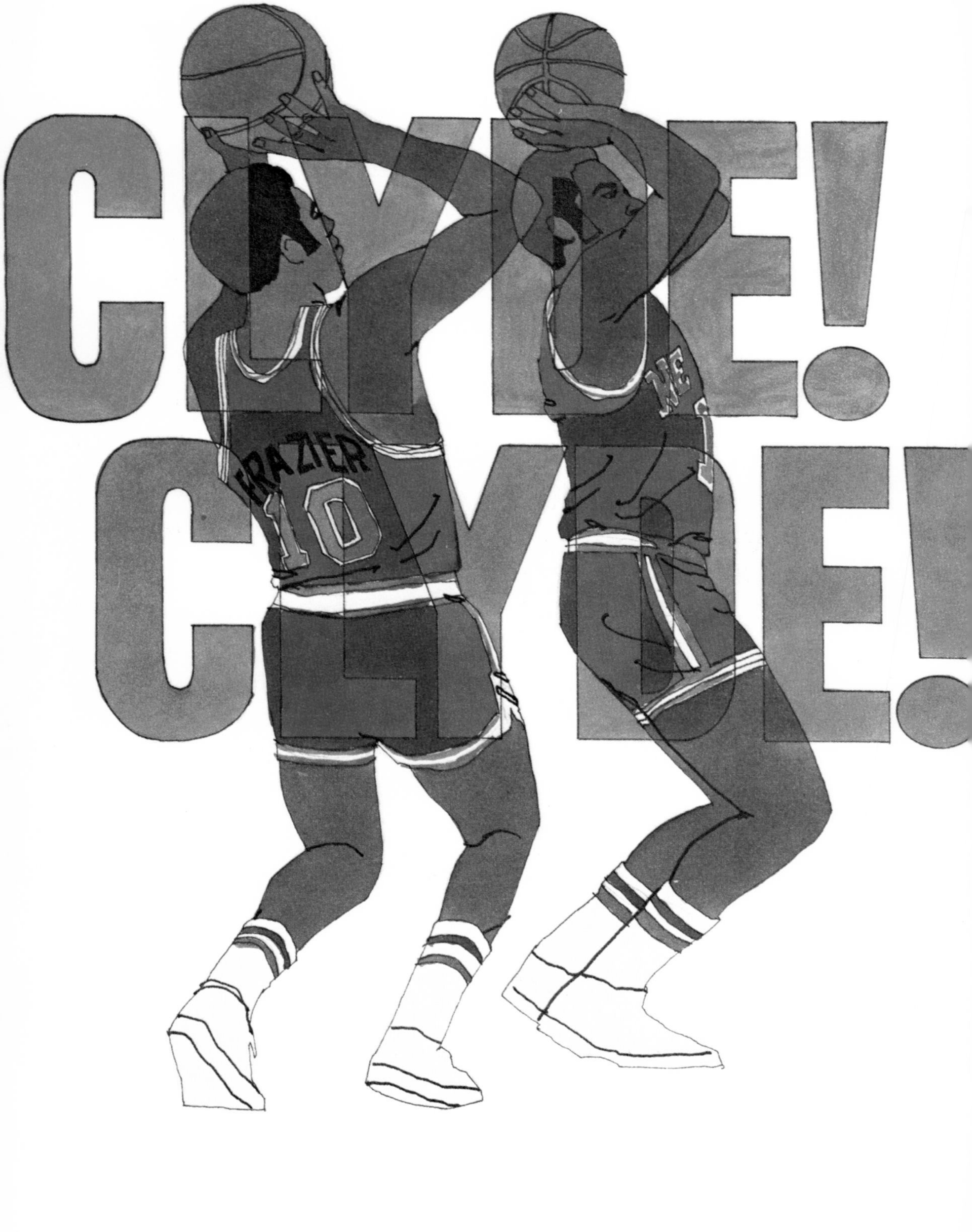
CLYDE!
CLYDE!
FRAZIER
10

Frazier has the fastest hands in basketball, many observers say. "He could swipe the hubcaps off a speeding car," a teammate once joked. As a Cincinnati player tried to pass the ball in, Frazier's hands blurred, blocking every angle. A dozen times the opponent started to pass, then drew back as Frazier anticipated the move.

At last, the Cincinnati player did what Frazier hoped for. He lobbed a high pass across court. A Knicks player intercepted and dribbled down the court for an easy layup. The Knicks trailed by only one point, 105 to 104. Thirteen seconds remained.

The Royals brought the ball down the court carefully. They didn't want to shoot since that would give the Knicks a chance to rebound. Knowing that, New York's Willis Reed gambled. He left his man to slap at the ball as a Royal dribbled near him. Reed batted the ball into a tangle of players.

Frazier's quick hands gathered it in. He drove downcourt and shot — but missed because a desperate Cincinnati player fouled him from behind. Frazier had three chances to make two free throws and give the Knicks that record-breaking 18th straight victory.

His first two shots swished through the net

without touching the hoop!

Frazier has a lively sense of humor. After the game he pretended to be astonished and a little bit angry when people asked him whether the pressure bothered him as he shot those free throws.

"Of course not," he said. "I wouldn't have had it any other way." Later on he dropped his pose, laughed and admitted: "If I'd missed, I wouldn't have had the nerve to come back to the locker room."

Basketball is the major sport of New York's playgrounds and schools. Children play it 12 months of the year. They learn the fine points of the game at an early age and become shrewd, demanding fans. They appreciate an all-around player more than one who is merely a fine shooter or a flashy ball-handler. When Frazier developed into a superstar in every phase of the game, he became the city's most popular sports hero.

Although New Yorkers regard Frazier as their kind of guy, he never even saw the city until his last season of college play. He was so awed that he would walk only in a straight line from his team's hotel for fear of getting lost if he turned a corner. Walt celebrated on that first trip by buying a shirt for $6, a huge sum to him at the time. Nowadays, a friend remarked, he often carries handkerchiefs that cost more.

Frazier was born March 29, 1945, in Atlanta, Georgia. He was the oldest child and has 7 sisters and a brother. Walt helped care for his sisters and with the housework. It was a great relief, he says, when some of his sisters grew up enough to take over changing diapers.

Most professional basketball players have concentrated on the game from early childhood. Frazier is an exception. He played whatever game was in season in Atlanta, starred in all of them, and enjoyed them all. He was a catcher in baseball, quarterback in football, and played every position in basketball.

Frazier learned to play basketball on dirt playgrounds. It was hard to dribble, especially after a rain when there would be holes and bumps and puddles. Despite the handicaps, Walt mastered the ball-handling skills that later amazed coaches and players in college and on the professional level. He learned to dribble equally well with either hand. By the time he was a 4th grader he could dribble behind his back and change directions without losing speed. He had also learned never to look at the ball, for that was the surest way

to have it stolen.

David T. Howard High School is an old brick building near the center of downtown Atlanta. An all-black school when Walt enrolled, it had been named for a black undertaker, the only man who would bury black people, Frazier explained in his book, CLYDE. He added that "if you weren't allowed to live in style, at least you could be planted in style."

Walt made the high school varsity team as a sophomore, playing center. The game he remembers

most vividly is his first one. He warmed up in his sweat suit and when the coach told him to go into the game, Walt pulled down his sweat pants only to discover that he had forgotten to put on his trunks. He had to run to the locker room.

"Every time I think about that game, it gets a little drafty in the room," Frazier once said.

Walt moved to guard in his junior year and the team didn't lose a regular season game that year or the next.

Walt was even better in football than in basketball. He could throw the ball 70 yards. Once when an opponent grabbed his right arm, Walt switched the ball to his left hand and completed the pass.

When he wasn't playing some game, Walt worked. He and a friend had jobs for two years at a drive-in. They used their savings to buy a 1949-model car that Walt remembers almost never ran. Even when it did, it sometimes caused him trouble. Atlanta bootleggers liked to soup up the same model car and use it to haul illegal whiskey. Often when Walt drove home at night, police would stop him and search his car.

There is no doubt in the minds of coaches who saw him in high school that Walt could have starred as a quarterback in college and professional football. But there were two obstacles. First, Walt hadn't been a good student. His grades weren't good enough for admission to Indiana and Kansas universities, which wanted him to play two sports. Second, Walt knew there were no black quarterbacks in pro football and he hoped for a professional career. He decided to concentrate on basketball.

He accepted a scholarship to Southern Illinois University, a then little-known school. Frazier helped change that, but it wasn't easy. Walt had a lot of problems to solve in those 4 years. He had a lot of growing up to do. He had trouble with his teammates, with his school work, and with himself. He sulked, loafed, lost his athletic eligibility, and finally quit school for a while.

During his sophomore year, Walt was averaging 19 points a game while an older and more popular player was averaging 20. Frazier wanted to be the scoring leader. His teammates felt that he was hotdogging, as players call it, and they decided to freeze him out of the scoring title by not passing to him very much.

Walt became even more of a loner. He skipped classes and sat alone in his room, watching television until late in the night. He lied to Coach Jack Hartman, telling him that he was going to class and having no trouble there. Then the grades came out and Walt was not eligible to play. The coach was angry. Walt was ashamed and embarrassed at having lied. He packed and went home to Atlanta. It appeared that his athletic career was over.

But Frazier was maturing. He realized that he was responsible for most of his problems. He decided to return to SIU even though he would have to pay his own way for a year until he could improve his grades. Then his scholarship would be restored.

He worked that summer in a cotton mill, pushing huge bales around. He wore weights on his legs to make it tougher and sometimes worked 12 hours a day. When a foreman learned that he was a college student, he offered Walt an easier job, but Frazier refused. He wanted to be in the best possible physical condition.

Back in school in the fall of 1965 he enrolled in difficult courses — history, math, science and worked hard. His grades improved. One thing he is most proud of is that he never again fell below a B in any course.

The 1965-1966 season was when he learned to love to play defense. He couldn't play with the varsity team or travel with it. But he could play defense day after day against the varsity. Frazier became so good that often the coach would pull him out of the practice so that the varsity players could regain their confidence.

"Coach Hartman treated me hard," Frazier said. "He didn't cut any corners for me, didn't do me any favors, and I didn't want him to."

Frazier began dating another Southern Illinois

student that year and they were married. The following year, his wife, Marsha, gave birth to a son, named Walt Frazier III. Frazier and his wife later were divorced, but Walt's love for his son is strong. He visits him at every opportunity.

"When I knocked on the nursery window and the nurse said, 'It's a boy,' and held him up, I think that was my proudest moment," Walt has said.

Southern Illinois lost just one game when Walt returned to the team for the 1966-1967 season. The team wasn't tall but played terrific defense. "It's not how tall you stand," Coach Hartman told them. "It's how tall you play."

At the end of the season, Southern Illinois was invited to play in the National Invitation Tournament in Madison Square Garden. Most New Yorkers had never heard of the school and, at first, they were more interested in the team's nickname than its players. "What is a Saluki?" sportswriters asked. They were told that it is an Egyptian hunting dog, very swift, perhaps the oldest pure breed in the world. The region around Carbondale, Illinois, where Southern Illinois University is located, is called Little Egypt.

When the tournament started, fans began talking

about the Salukis' players, especially Frazier. He captivated them with his variety of skills and clutch plays. The Salukis won the tournament, destroying Marquette in the finals, 71-56. Walt was named the tournament's Most Valuable Player. He had scored 88 points and had 24 rebounds and 11 assists. He was the team's playmaker, too, and his passing was as important as his shooting.

Red Holzman, chief scout for the Knicks, watched the tournament. He was convinced that Frazier was the man needed to pull the Knicks' many fine players together into a smoothly working team. He persuaded the Knicks' executives to make Walt their No. 1 draft choice in 1967.

Frazier could be drafted by the National Basketball Association (NBA) because his original class was graduating. When he was chosen in the first round by New York, Walt decided to pass up the year of college ball he had remaining and sign a pro contract.

Neither man has ever regretted it. Holzman was named coach of the Knicks in December of 1967. He put together their famous pressing defense and controlled offense and Frazier became the team's floor leader, just as Holzman had predicted.

In 1970, after the Knicks won the first National Basketball Association championship in the team's history, team captain Willis Reed let the public know how important Frazier was to the team.

"On the Knicks, the ball belongs to Frazier," Reed said. "He just lets us play with it sometimes."

It didn't happen overnight. As a rookie Frazier played poorly until Holzman had a quiet talk with him.

"You're a better player than you're showing," Holzman told Walt. "I want you to start thinking basketball. We need you."

"Thinking" was the key word. It snapped Frazier out of his bad habits and he began paying attention to the game. When he was sent in, he would know the situation and what he should contribute.

One night everything fell together. The Knicks were losing to Los Angeles because nobody could stop a hot-shooting Laker guard. The Knicks were also missing their own outside shots and were having trouble passing the ball in to their high scorer, Willis Reed.

Frazier went in at halftime and held that Laker guard scoreless the rest of the game. "He got inside his shirt," as players say when someone does a great job on defense. Frazier also passed magnificently, getting

8 assists, mostly on perfect passes to Reed. And he took 6 jump shots from outside the foul circle and hit 5 of them!

"Way to go, Walt," a teammate shouted in the locker room. "You're our Johnny Unitas."

Red Holzman heard and nodded with satisfaction. His team needed a "quarterback" and he was happy to see the players turning to Frazier for leadership.

The Knicks finished third in Frazier's first 2 seasons, but they were becoming a better team all the time and Frazier was acquiring new skills himself. For instance, he began driving to the basket — even against the huge, terrifyingly-strong Laker center, Wilt Chamberlain.

"The first time Frazier did it, I closed my eyes," Willis Reed once said. "I didn't want to see what Wilt was going to do to him."

But Frazier ducked Chamberlain's pile-driving arm and scored. He kept driving at every opportunity. It was one more thing for opponents to worry about. As if Walt's defense, passing, dribbling, and outside shooting weren't enough!

In Frazier's second year, NBA coaches voted him on an all-defensive team. The coaches were the first to recognize that Frazier was probably the finest defensive guard in the modern history of the game.

Any analysis of Frazier's game must start with defense. He frustrates opponents' attempts to shoot and pass. He also turns defense into an offensive weapon by stealing the ball more often than any other player in the game.

Walt hounds opponents tirelessly, his body balanced with one foot ahead of the other and his hands medium high. He seldom touches an opponent since many shooters depend on a shove to give them direction. They react to the push by whirling away and shooting.

"I like to leave a man hanging suspended in the air, waiting to be whacked," Walt explained once. "It psychs him. I call it phantom defense. He never knows for sure where I am, but if he does turn to shoot, I have a hand in front of his face."

Frazier's steals depend as much on timing and careful study of his opponent's habits as on his fast hands. He never grabs the ball. He slaps it away and more times than not, one of Walt's teammates will retrieve it.

"Clyde will steal the ball from his man early in the game," Knicks forward Bill Bradley said once, "and after that he'll just flick his hand and you'll see the man flinch."

When guarding a man with the ball, Frazier tries to force him to go where he is least effective. If the man likes to drive down the middle, Walt forces him to the side of the court. If he prefers to shoot from the left side, Walt forces him inside or to the

right. Some players are "spot" shooters, deadly accurate from a particular spot on the floor. Frazier knows that and works to keep them away from that spot.

When a shot is in the air, Frazier boxes his man out — getting between him and the basket. That is easier said than done. Pro basketball is an extremely rough game. Frazier is 6 feet, 4 inches tall, weighs 205

pounds, and is unusually strong. Even so, he often is the smallest man on the floor. When he tries to get position for a rebound, he is battered by the arms, elbows and hips of 2 or 3 larger men. Still Walt averages 500 rebounds a year, twice as many as a lot of guards.

The quickness and poise that make Frazier a superstar on defense are just as important on offense. Coaches say that dribbling a ball around a man who is trying to take it away is the single hardest thing a basketball player is called upon to do. That is Frazier's first duty on offense.

"My job is to penetrate, to get inside the opponent's outer line," Frazier once explained. "If I do that, they have to move a man out of position to stop me."

When an opponent moves out of position, it leaves a Knick player unguarded for an instant. Frazier's pass will find that man. If no one comes out to stop him, Walt keeps driving and shoots. He hits 50 percent of his shots. Many times he turns a basket into a 3-point play by drawing a foul as he shoots. Frazier hits 80 percent of his free throws. Opponents know they can't afford to foul him, but often they can't help it.

If he can penetrate the defense, Frazier keeps moving the ball around. He tries to pass to a teammate and move to screen for him so he can get a shot away. Or he looks for mismatches — such as a short guard on a tall Knick front court player. Mismatches occur when players switch assignments on defense. The Knicks' offense is designed to force many defensive switches.

These maneuvers are performed at full speed because a pro team must shoot the ball within 24 seconds or lose it. That is one reason many teams rely on a fast-break offense. They don't have a playmaker like Frazier who can set up a basket within the time limit.

Frazier would rather have an assist — a pass to a player who scores — than a basket. He has proved that many times and his unselfishness has been called the key to the Knicks' attack. However, when necessary, Frazier can score with the best. He averages a little over 20 points a game even though he seldom shoots very much when his teammates are hitting. His points come in clusters when the Knicks need them the most. Once he scored his team's last 13 points to bring them from behind to beat the Milwaukee Bucks 101 to 99.

Frazier is not a flashy shooter. He makes scoring look easy by doing precisely the right thing at the right instant. He can switch the ball from one hand to another in mid-air, if necessary, and even makes that look simple.

"You can't steal the ball from him and you can't block his shot," an opponent once grumbled. "You need a gun to stop the man."

But Frazier's trademark is the clutch play. Such as the game in which he stole the ball 8 times as the Knicks came from behind to defeat Atlanta.

Then there was the famous "one-second play" at Detroit. The Knicks trailed 111 to 110 with one second showing on the clock. They had the ball out of bounds near the middle of the court and Frazier had to pass it in, knowing that the clock would start the instant a player on the court touched the ball. Walt threw it perfectly more than half the length of the court to a point just over the rim. Willis Reed, who is 6 feet 10 inches tall, leaped high and stuffed the ball through the net as the buzzer sounded.

Detroit fans sat in stunned silence as Frazier ran off the court laughing.

Perhaps his most important clutch performance came in 1970 when the Knicks won the National Basketball Association title. An original member of the NBA, the Knicks had been playing since 1946, but had never won the championship. The final 1970 playoff series with Los Angeles was tied at 3 games apiece.

The Knicks had to play the deciding game without Reed, who was injured. The Knick's only chance was to shoot well from the outside and to keep the ball away from the Lakers' gigantic Wilt Chamberlain.

"Clyde" rose to the occasion. He scored 36 points, had 19 assists, and stole the ball 5 times. The Knicks won 113 to 99.

After the game, Frazier was asked to describe his own performance. He didn't hesitate an instant.

"I was dynamite!" he said. Fans who heard or read the remark roared with laughter. That was just what they had been thinking.

Since that night, "Clyde" has continued to be dynamite on the court and off. He led the Knicks to another NBA title in 1973 and has been an All-Star team selection every year.

Today Frazier is one of New York's true celebrities. He receives about 500 letters a day and is recognized everywhere. He is a millionaire — a cool million, of course. He has a long term contract with the Knicks for a reported $250,000 a year. He owns all or part of several businesses and operates a summer boys camp where he keeps in condition.

He owns a home in Atlanta in which his mother

lives and another in upstate New York. In the city, he lives in a 5-room penthouse apartment which cost $25,000 to decorate. In his closets there is an elegant wardrobe including more than 50 suits and 100 pairs of shoes. His clothes are a bit more conservative than when he received his nickname, but "Clyde" still attracts attention in one of his two sealskin coats or one of elephant hide.

He drives a 1965 Rolls Royce because he prefers its styling to that of the later models. He pays $140 a month for two parking stalls and parks in the middle to prevent scratches and dents.

But he is a basketball player first. Everything else comes second. Although he never plays basketball during the summer, he runs at least 2 miles every morning and works with weights regularly. When training camp opens, he is ready to play.

Recently the Knicks were making a television commercial. There were several stacks of scripts. The players were told to pick one that fit them. The various scripts were marked "For High Scorers," "For Defensive Stars," "For Passing Aces," and so on.

"Hey," somebody shouted, "Clyde better take one of each."

JACK NICKLAUS
BILL RUSSELL
MARK SPITZ
VINCE LOMBARDI
BILLIE JEAN KING
ROBERTO CLEMENTE
JOE NAMATH
BOBBY HULL
HANK AARON
JERRY WEST
TOM SEAVER
JACKIE ROBINSON
MUHAMMAD ALI
O. J. SIMPSON
JOHNNY BENCH
WILT CHAMBERLAIN
ARNOLD PALMER
A. J. FOYT

superstars!
superstars
superstars

JOHNNY UNITAS
GORDIE HOWE
WALT FRAZIER
PHIL AND TONY ESPOSITO
BOB GRIESE
FRANK ROBINSON
PANCHO GONZALES
LEE TREVINO
KAREEM ABDUL JABBAR
JEAN CLAUDE KILLY
EVONNE GOOLAGONG
ARTHUR ASHE